SAQIBISM

ARIELLE& LOUIS

WITH ALL MY LOVE.
HAVE A BLESSED LIFE

SAQIB
11/15/20

SAQIBISM

Poems & Quotes

Saqib Rasool

ISBN-13: 9781097198399

Dedication

In the loving memory of Mian Faiz Rasool, Ch. Pervaiz Bashir, and Dr. James McManis, who set examples for me to go beyond one's default circumstances and boldly explore new worlds and new horizons—whose kindness could bore a hole in the heart of a mountain.

To the souls that long to resurrect, hunt injustice, and manifest beauty in our worlds.

Contents

Foreword

I met Saqib at a time when our lives were both in great turmoil. Although at that time this turmoil seemed to have been generated by external events, through innumerable evenings of deep, honest, open conversations we were able not only to discover the roots of suffering within ourselves, but also examine the multiple facets of the experience of being human through reexamination of the tenets of many philosophies and religions.

Our conversations would at times travel mysteriously from one subject to another in a haphazard way, but always held together by the thread of curiosity, discovery and love for the truth, be this relative or absolute. Those conversations were only the starting point for both of us to continue our journeys independently, each armed only with the pure desire of finding our own true self.

This collection is the result of Saqib's personal journey. In it, I find faint reflections of those early days of sleepless nights filled with the rare essence of naked thought, all elaborated and lyrically expressed along the unique path of reflections and intuitions of my good friend.

I am sure the reader will find this collection very entertaining and deeply meaningful at the same time, as Saqib's personal experiences are elaborated and expressed through a fabulous mix of mysticism, tongue-in-cheek humor and disarming directedness.

Sit back and enjoy the experience.

Bruno Alabiso
Former Microsoft Researcher & Eclectic

Preface

Saqibism is the only "ism" that cannot be followed. I abhor all isms. My sincerest wish is that, that anyone who reads this will develop their own internal compass—their own *ism*. My friend and mentor, James, often said, if you are worth your salt, you will not walk another's path but make your own, and I agree. Through life experiences, I found this to be true for the inner spiritual journey and the process of bringing forth new and important innovations to the world. If you are copying others you are not living your full potential that nature has bestowed each human being with.

Everything I have written here has occurred to me as an insight while dealing with my own struggles and through the close involvement in the struggles of my loved ones. If you find one of my fingers pointing at you, you can trust that all the rest are pointing at my own self. In that manner, everything I have said, I have experienced it for myself within the framework of my own life.

Many of these writings are extremely personal to me and I have only published them upon the insistence of my dear friend, and the editor of this book, Victoria Ruelas, and to whom I owe a great deal of gratitude.

I thank all my teachers, for the innumerable gifts and experiences that reflect in these writings, starting with my mother, Parveen Bashir, and my father, Faiz Rasool, and then my siblings, Aqib, Nadia, Amara, and particularly Muneeb for being the mirrors of my soul. I also thank my childhood friends, Sohail Anwar, Abu-Bakr, Zahid, Tayyab, Fida, Umar, and Sajjad; my cousins, Kashi bhai, Rabia, Goshi, and Faisal, and aunts, Naseem Khala Jan, and Zahida Api Jan, for the foundational experiences upon which the tree of my life would grow.

I am in debt to all my early mentors, starting with Hakeem Saeed, and then Mrs. Peter, Ikram Bhutta, Pasha, and Sheikh Zahid; and then Steve Pepitone, and Garret Jacobs, who taught me important early lessons.

I especially thank my dear friends Bruno Alabiso and Chauncey Bell, who shared their lives and gifts so generously with me, making a profound impact on my trajectory.

Chauncey introduced me to Fernando Flores.

I thank Fernando Flores, who opened a new sensibility in me about our shared existence and taught me that *entrepreneurship is public service*. Meeting Fernando has been the most important milestone for me.

And an acknowledgment to Allama Iqbal and Roberto Mangabeira Unger whose works have been lighting a fire in my heart and with whom I share the dream of the transformation of mankind.

And with deep gratitude to S.N. Goenka and Sadhguru Jaggi Vasudev who taught me meditation and the Yogic and Vedic philosophy.

Lastly to all my loved ones and friends (who have listened so patiently to me over the years) including Sonia Ruelas, Syed Mehdi, Tehsin Khan, Fumei Sung, Yilei Wang, Maureen Daniek, Maudi Alabiso, Touseef Liaqat, Kunal Mahajan, Rosemeri Reinehr, Lara Dubugras, Reika Sasano, Akash Maharaj, Andy McBride, Michele Gazzolo, Darrel Rhea, Gil Friend, Mark Raymond, Ron Kaufman, Jim Myers, Mihir Rao, Rochelle Moulton, Shifu Zhou, Rob Matthewson, Nick Karnik, Katie Brennecke, and everyone else that I have not mentioned here, I thank you also.

This note of thanks would not be complete without my gratitude to Coleman Barks who brought me to Rumi. It is through Barks' articulation of Rumi I would re-discover the soul of Islam.

My claim is that, in this book, there is a page just for you. If you find it, it will be more precious than any other material gift you have ever received.

Follow nothing I say blindly and see it for yourself. The goal is the awakening of your own inner teacher.
I wish you the very best on your journey.

Saqib Rasool
Seattle, May 6th, 2019

My God! Open up for me my heart.
And ease for me my task.
And untie the knot of my tongue.
That they may understand my speech.

The Prayer of Moses, Qur'an

This Is Saqibism

If you are a Muslim, be a good Muslim.
If you are a Hindu, be a good Hindu.
If you are a Buddhist, be a good Buddhist.

If you are a Christian, you have a mission;
to be a good Christian, to be a good Christian.

Be a good Daoist.
Be a good Marxist.
Be a good Capitalist.
Be a good Socialist.

But if you a fundamentalist, you better see an
herbalist.

Be a good human and don't be a horrible.
Better read your Geeta and better read your
Bible.

But, if you become irresponsible.
And make life terrible.
Your family is miserable.
Your treatment unbearable.
Your acts less than honorable.
Then you are just an asshole.

Love makes us live extraordinary lives.

Quit negotiating others' legends and unfold your own.

For an entrepreneur, the program of building a powerful enterprise must begin with a program of building a powerful self.

An entrepreneurial mind wants possibilities and openings; an employee mind certainty and guarantees. It's a matter of choice.

You Are the World

The world has been kind.
The world has been lame.
The world is divine.
The world is profane.
The world is a cold reality.
The world is a hot illusion.
The world is straight up.
The world is a freaking confusion.
The world is a game.
The world is not to blame.
The world is a mirror.
And the mirror has your name.

The world.
Wake up and she is yours.

The Experience of Enlightenment

The clock of *Vipassana* struck and it happened.

When it happens;
all time merges into one.
You can see all the way to the future and all the
way back.
Your identity is blown into a million billion
pieces fused with everything else in the
universe.
All are experienced as one.
All space too merges into one.
One is experienced as all.

It is as if trillions and centillions of images are
downloaded in your brain and you are present to
all of them simultaneously.

There is no philosophy that can explain what it
is.
It can only be experienced.

It is physical and real.
Becoming aware of what you really are;
Presence.

It is a rift in space and time.

Like a crack in an old door; Gateway to infinite
knowledge.

Experiencing it, is a human possibility.

Enlightenment begins when mind fully understands, that the power who made it, dwells within it.

Equanimous awareness creates paths to liberation.

It's a moment of surrender, when the mind says, you have shown me the logic of your presence, now you take me.

Purpose

Begin your day with *Fajr* and end with *Isha*.
Resurrect your sleeping soul.
Give up chasing your urgent wanting.
Hunt injustice and bring light to the world.

Fajr - morning meditation
Isha - evening meditation

With a blindfold of devotion, tyrants seize power by constructing fake monsters and vowing to fight them.

The story of Hussein teaches us that no matter how big a tyrant—you must speak the truth—no matter the price.

Changemakers

So, you want to do a startup, be an artist, start a movement, change things?
Very well.
Know this, you will be the master of your destiny.
You will grow beyond you can imagine.
You will love your life and won't have another way.
You will not be a slave.
But things will not go like you planned.
You will know pain like you have never before.
Your worst nightmare will come true.
You go against the grain and the usual and the normal.
No one will appreciate anything you have done.
You will be alone.
But there is a success, progress, and an evolution.
To succeed, you must find a heart and learn to experiment.
Learn from each attempt.
Value failure more than success.
Success gets you drunk and mindless.
Failure teaches you what does not work.
So, you can find what works and make life better.
You will succeed.

It's a hard line to walk.
Actually, there is no line.

In a struggle for building better worlds, imagination and courage are the sword and shield of entrepreneurs.

Do not think much about how to accumulate.
Spend your time thinking about how to create.

An entrepreneur is not someone who plans to become something. An entrepreneur is someone who lives his or her possibility in each moment.

Innovation comes from paying attention to anomalies, and not by constructing perfect plans and visions.

"Planning" works for known, stable and recurring futures. For futures unknown and unstable, *planning* is useless.

Innovation begins with gripping a serious dissatisfaction that is felt but ignored by others as common sense. Innovation then is about inventing and delivering a new satisfaction.

Hunger is not a resource issue.
Hunger is a coordination issue.

Whatever you think stands in your way to success, is actually your bridge to success.

Success comes from the slavery of your word.

Entrepreneurship is the skill of coping with and
harvesting opportunities from change.
Innovation is the habit that differentiates the
living from the extinct.

Hyperactivity is neither management nor leadership. It is an ailment of the nervous system that can destroy any project.

The Club of Alchemists

The right question is not that who is making all
this work.
The right question is what is making all this
work.
The question is not who you are.
The question is what you are.

If I say money, there is money.

If your head escapes your skull and flies to stars
and beyond,
        it is because your alchemist soul feeds on
the nectar of enlightenment.

Many times, I have this feeling since I have
been with you.
I cannot describe it.
Plow, plow, and plow.

So;
what is the work of an Alchemist?
Bring people to new futures.
Open wormholes.
Just this kind of stuff.

Our worlds are in trouble because we have outsourced the job of thinking, to a group called Analysts.

Your life will explode with greatness,
when you fall in love,
with the hidden intelligence,
that runs your body and your mind.

You are either a victim of transformation or you are a source of transformation. It's up to you.

Human Being is a game set up by God so that
God realizes God is God.

The Choice of Freedom

I saw a dream,
where I was given a choice to surrender.

I did not want to.
I liked being a rebel.
I liked being free.
Except that I wasn't free—
held by nothing but my illusions.

I had eyes but I couldn't see.
I couldn't see because I had no vision.
I had no vision because I didn't know.

And when that knowledge came to me,
I was truly free.

That freedom was in a surrender
of the illusion of becoming free.

Surrender of,
getting this and getting that,
having this and having that,
wanting this and wanting that.

I worked hard to be free,
but the more I tried the more happiness flee.

This dilemma was made clear,
in a dream that was like a river.

I saw a dream,
where I was given a choice to surrender.

Cultivating care for others is the key to living a successful and satisfying life.

Wake Up

At night Beloved comes to me,
and tells me to wake up,
and clean up the holy place,
and make good on my annunciations,
and proclamations,
of being in love with the Mystery.

My Beloved is a sun.
Too close, I burn.
Too far, I whither.

The Real Gift

I will chase you till the edge of the universe,
till the end of time.

When you'll be a star,
I will become stardust.

When you will be a planet,
I will be your moon.

Where you are, there I am.

We will never meet.
We will never split.

You didn't give me home.
You gave me longing for home.
The gift you gave me is better than a union.
The real gift is the agony of separation.

The darkness within darkness wills things,
and atoms split with awe.

Every tragedy in my life has turned out to be a blessing. Blessing or tragedy it's just a matter of view; isn't it?

Tragedy has a way of bringing clarity.

Breakfast

I don't live for the breakfast.
I live for the taste of the breakfast that lives in
me.

*A note: Since I was young, my mother made me an
English breakfast every day before school; two eggs, a
toast, and a cup of tea. After coming to the United States,
for the last 25 years, I have made for myself and eaten
mostly the same breakfast. Sometimes I fast and eat my
first meal in the afternoon. It does not matter when I eat
my first meal, it is this. Victoria once teasingly said,
'Saqib lives only for his breakfast'. These two lines
occurred in response.*

Men who think women cannot be leaders are not happily married.

The root of man's violence towards women is his refusal to honor women's choices.

Men and women have forgotten how to be with each other. What most are left with are domination-games and remembrance of a wounded self.

The Prayer of The Lambs

Close the butchery Ya Sufi.
Eat the veggies Ya Sufi.
Change the *dhara* Ya Sufi.
Find *kinara* Ya Sufi.
Dard humara Ya Sufi.
Dard humara Ya Sufi.
Close the butchery Ya Sufi.
Eat the veggies Ya Sufi.

All the times you are hungry.
Your addiction is the meat.
Close the butchery Ya Sufi.
Eat the veggies Ya Sufi.

We die in millions every day.
Kept in boxes, kept away.

Close the butchery Ya Sufi.
Eat the veggies Ya Sufi.

dhara = direction
kinara = shoreline
dard humara = our pain

Taking anything from nature without
compassion is *haram*.

When you live among corrupts, you will not easily know the difference between good and evil.

Not the First Time

This is not the first time we have fallen from grace.

Being in love is a sickness.
Only the sick like it.
To outsiders, it appears a loser's game.

No gain with irrational thinking?
Yeah right—For a lover a single kiss of beloved,
is worth more than a billion mines of sparkling diamonds.

Then it was clear to me Akash Maharaj—
The size of your life and your work depends on the size of what you love.

Say those words to my ear my love and let us walk together into the eternal garden.

To see the evil in others one must begin with locating that evil within oneself.

The secret to a joyous life is to do nothing secretly at all.

To All the Angry Beings

This how you are,
is not your fault, or your responsibility.
This is rather an opportunity;
a new possibility.

What you think stands between you and your
goals, is not your enemy but a bridge.

This anger is your bride.
Misuse her and she will ruin your old-age.
Ignore her and she will set fire to your house.
Tame her and she will pleasure you forever.

Selfishness begets selfishness. Deceit begets
deceit. Unkindness invites misery.

If you are angry about not getting what you
want,
wait till you find out what was hidden from your
wanting.

Enlightenment is rarely gotten
      by chasing elusive mystics!

Happiness is never gotten
      by occupying pretty dwellings!

Satisfaction is not found
      by forcing your will on others.

Chauncey tells me about an American
tradition—to keep children occupied, they are
told to hunt for the Snipe bird.

And they hunt ceaselessly.

Except for that, the Snipe bird does not exist.

We have been children; tricked, busied.

Give up your hunt.
And then see what is really worth hunting.

Forgiveness is a master move one can make in the game of life to gain a clear visible advantage.

Love and kindness is the best strategy.

The sooner you give up calculating life,
the sooner joy starts entering life.

Your life will explode with greatness if you change, *'why is this happening to me,'* to, *'why am I doing this to myself.'*

Dear sky, have mercy on us,
and deliver us from our temptations,
as what appears to be freedom,
is a wide road to hell.

This Too Will Change

What is up, will go down.
What is down, will come up.
What is now, it never was.
What was once, will never be.

Watch with awe my sweet child;
how the world unfolds in front of your eyes.

And what's behind the eyes is a vast mystery.

Don't sell the self in greed for something tasty
or in fear of something nasty.

The first step to enlightenment is letting go of the need to defend your religion.

When upon hearing something wise you are quick to put it in a box called, *'my book has everything'*, you learn neither from your book nor from what's being said.

Humility comes from disappearing the sense of entitlement. Humility is then taking full responsibility for your gifts.

Compulsive and obsessive identification with your looks, intelligence, lineage, and assets, is the root of all your suffering.

All failure in life is a failure of listening.

Ego is a cloth for you to wear.
When your clothes wear you, you are in trouble.

Absorption of thoughts creates slavery
and observation of senses freedom.

Thresholds

Mental models create affixations in the minds of their creators.

Threshold after threshold.
I cross one and there is another one waiting.
But I am that I am.
I must cross them all.

And sit at each as a dog sits at the house door,
waiting to be let in;
waiting patiently, fervently, constantly,
never giving up.

Innovate or Die

You are big and strong and mean.
You work hard and you are dedicated.
You have been around a long time.
But you see an asteroid coming.
You see the sky turning dark.
It is time to grow wings and fly.
It is time to—innovate or die.

Experience and experiment are the same thing.
If you want experience you must experiment.

(The Urdu language uses the same word for the
both called *tajarba* تجربہ)

Manifestation Process

To manifest something,
four conditions must be true.

You must want it.
You must deserve it.
You must need it.
You must believe it.

Common sense is a coffin.

The relentless pursuit of keeping up with the new stuff is a widespread mental disease on the planet.

Understanding—a blessing and a curse. Just because you have avoided the next pothole, you think you know the way. No, you don't.

Friday Evening

That fleeting period of time,
when you briefly feel,
that everything is going to be okay.

Friday evening.

All you need to do today is to fall in love with life.

In A Room Full of Dogs, You Are A Bag Full of Catnip

Disaster after disaster.
Heartbreak after heartbreak.
Your love denied.
Your secrets pried.
You endlessly cried.

Your heart is broken.
Your country is stolen.
Who did this?
We did this. I did this. You did this.
Who did this?

Your reputation ruined.
Your offerings rejected.
Your enemies selected.

Angels turned devils.
You're thrown below levels.

Your movements clocked.
Your poems mocked.
Your art blocked.

Disaster after disaster.
Heartbreak after heartbreak.

You get the goats not for their opinions but for their meat. Such is the mood of the job markets today.

Take Your Medicine

You have already invented,
the perfect medicine,
that you need,
for your kind of madness.

Now you take it.
And do what needs to be done.

If you take it,
and do what needs to be done,
you will be free, and experience this deep
freedom,
that is more precious than all the beautiful
things you want so much.

If you cannot take this medicine,
then leave this gathering,
return to your ancestral home,
and wait to die.

You have already invented,
the perfect medicine,
that you need,
for your kind of madness.

The evil that grows in the night;
it is better to kill it in the day.

If you only listen to what you understand,
you only learn what you already know.

You can only get well,
if you treat yourself like a sick person.

New Clothes

What you do and how you be,
     in the worst moments of your life,
     defines the quality of what comes after.

The thing that is stinging you now,
     is your own unfulfillable desire
unfulfilled,
     turned into a venomous scorpion sting.

The thing you want the most can never be
yours.
     The thing you really need, already is.

There is great freedom in letting go wanting
how you want it.

There is a mystery in all this.
It is the mystery that is above all teachings, all
sayings.

Give yourself to this and put on new clothes like
the *Eid day.*

Eid day - the day of a holy festival

Desire is like a balloon completely empty in its nature but puffed up only by emotions and feelings.

You can never become like anybody else.
You can only become you.

Life for most is a tragedy film with brief intermissions of happiness. Isn't it so?

The Illusion of Time

Mystery has spoken to you.
Why don't you listen?
A call has been made.
You don't belong here.
Your realm is different.
Seven mothers have called.
Seven fathers have called.
You still don't answer.
Destiny sits tired at your doorsteps.
Tired from knocking all day and all night.

Why are you still asleep?
Do you love your dreams so much that you won't
bring them to reality?

Listen, the Mystery is still speaking to you...
If you listen silently, you'll hear the whispers.

Anything that could be coherently understood as God, cannot be God.

Just a Little While Longer

It's interesting now,
that I used to stay awake,
for long hours.
I wanted to party,
I wanted to enjoy life,
and never sleep.
Now every time,
I pass by my bed,
around the evening time, it calls me.
I say to my bed,
I'm coming, I'm coming,
just a little while longer.

I do the same with my grave.
Every time that spot enters my mind,
I whisper to it,
I'm coming, I'm coming,
just a little while longer.

Supernova

When it has been dark too long;
light explodes in the heart of a star.

Everything is new.
Everywhere *Allah huuu!*

You must go,
      where your animal soul is afraid to go.

The Vortex is Opening

The time has come.
All lineages are connected.
All stars aligned.
All servants stand in line.
My God, the vortex is opening.

The time has come.

All realities converging.
All races stand united.
To face what is coming.

The vortex is opening.

Our doing could not be outrun.
There was no vigil.
No one stayed up all night.

The time unwrapped.
At the sorrow of the children.
And sent out a call.

And the call was answered.
And an account was taken.
Our doing could not be outrun.

Now the vortex is opening.
The judgment day prepares.
A different journey begins.

A philosopher becomes a teacher.
A soldier becomes a servant.
The humble becomes a king.

New realms open.
New possibilities emerging.
New adventures begin.

A new story is written.
A new lover is loved.
A new home with kin.

A new self emerges.
In the drifting eternity.
A man writes his destiny.

All mourning comes to an end.
All sins are forgiven.
The sixth Golden Age begins.

My God, the vortex is opening.

The measure of a successful conversation
is the space it opens for the next conversation.

About the Typefaces

This book was set in IM Fell for titles, and Century for the body.

Starting in the mid-16th century, the British monarchy interfered with printing technology preventing the development of typefounding in England. By 17th-century most type used by the English printers was of Dutch origin. This moved the Bishop of Oxford, Dr. John Fell to purchase punches & matrices from Holland c. 1670–1672 for use by the Oxford University Press. The Fell type is likely the work of a Dutch punchcutter Dirck Voskens, who sold it to Dr. John Fell. Fell type boasts short extenders, high stroke contrast, narrowing of round letters, and flattened serifs on the baseline and descenders. Open-Source digitization of the modern Fell Types was released by an Italian designer and civil engineer, Igino Marini, hence the name—IM Fell.

Century was invented by an American designer and inventor, Linn Boyd Benton, in 1894 for use in *The Century Magazine*. It was rapidly expanded into a large type family first by Linn Boyd and later by his son, Morris. Its design promotes elegance and crispness. In the 21st century, its use continues to remain strong in literature, textbooks, and journals. The Supreme Court of the United States requires that briefs be typeset in Century family type.

Notes

Notes

Notes

Notes

Made in the USA
Monee, IL
15 July 2020

35754508R20069